The KNOW-NONSENSE Guide to MEASUREMENTS

Written by Heidi Fiedler

Illustrated by Brendan Kearney

Quarto is the authority on a wide range of topics.
Quarto educates, entertains, and enriches the lives of our readers—
enthusiasts and lovers of hands-on living.
www.quartoknows.com

© 2017 Quarto Publishing Group USA Inc.
Published by Walter Foster Jr.,
an imprint of The Quarto Group
All rights reserved. Walter Foster Jr. is a registered trademark.

Text by Heidi Fiedler
Illustrations by Brendan Kearney

6 Orchard Road, Suite 100
Lake Forest, CA 92630
quartoknows.com
Visit our blogs at quartoknows.com

MIX
Paper from
responsible sources
FSC® C101537

Printed in China
1 3 5 7 9 10 8 6 4 2

TABLE OF CONTENTS

INTRODUCTION

If understanding **measurement** seems boring, or you're looking for a funny guide to measurement, you're in the right place. This book tackles the **key concepts** introduced in school that might be confusing the first time around.

- The metric system and closely related International System of Units (SI) are used by most people in the world. They include units like meters, liters, and grams.

- In the metric system, base units are given prefixes like *milli-*, *centi-*, and *kilo-*. Whatever unit you use, *milli-* means "thousandth," *centi-* means "hundredth," and *kilo-* means "thousand."

- Americans use a different system that includes inches, gallons, and pounds.

Sound like nonsense? Fear not! By the end of this book, you'll be ready to use units like **pints**, **AUs**, and **moles**, as well as know how to **convert** between the most common units. You might even be able to measure your own improvement!

LENGTH

How long is it? The tools and units you use to answer this question depend on the size of the object you're measuring.

Tape measures, rulers, and odometers all measure length or distance. Itty bitty things like star dust might be measured in millimeters, while super large, intergalactic distances are better measured with unusual (but useful) units like AUs. That's the long and short of it!

INCH & CENTIMETER

Units of length used to measure small objects

An **inch** is a unit of length we use nearly every day—at least in the United States. It's about the width of two of your fingers put together. Technically, it's 1/12 of a foot. Around the world, most people use the metric system. They measure short lengths using centimeters. A **centimeter** is 1/100 of a meter. It's roughly the width of one of your fingers. Using a ruler is the best way to measure how many inches or centimeters something is—whether it's a banana or a slug!

CENTIMETERS

0 1 2 3 4 5 6 7 8 9 10

0   1   2   3   4

INCHES

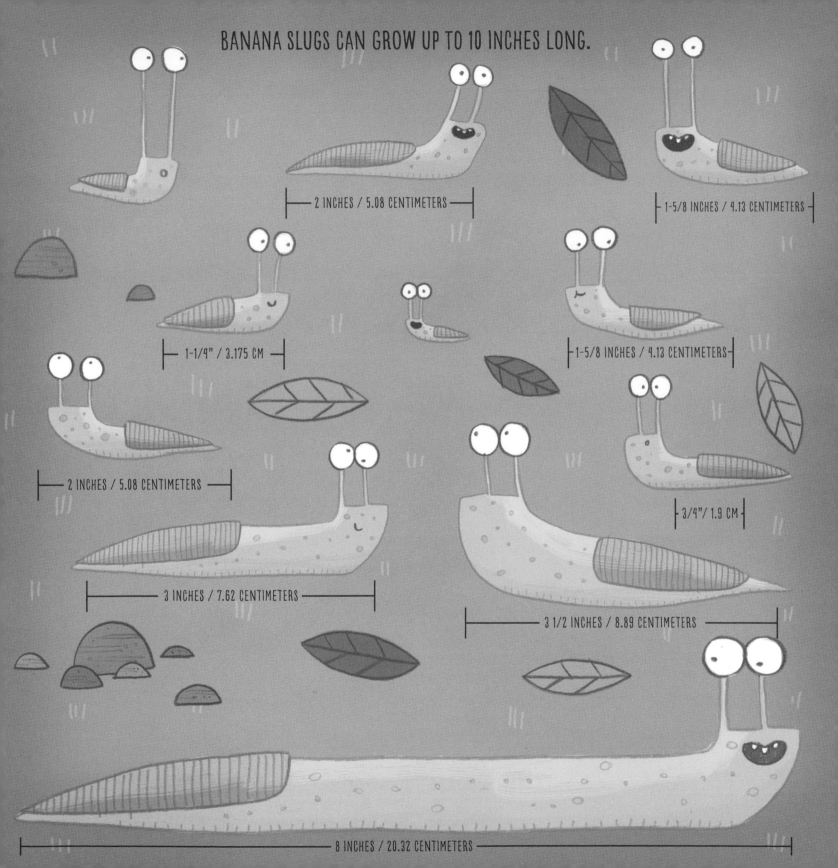

FOOT, METER & YARD

Units of length used to measure midsize distances

People come in all shapes and sizes. And so do units of length! The **meter** is the base unit of length in the International System of Units (SI), which is closely related to the metric system. All other units of length in these systems are based on the meter.

Americans use a different system that includes inches, feet, and yards to measure distances. There are 12 inches in a **foot**, and 3 feet in a **yard**. If you're in America, it helps to know a meter is 39.37 inches long. Historians think the foot was inspired by real human feet—though whether those feet were mini jockey feet or mondo basketball feet is still a mystery!

1 METER

1 YARD

1 FOOT

*LENGTH DRAWN TO SCALE, NOT ACTUAL SIZE

MILE & KILOMETER

Units of length used to measure large distances

Depending who you ask (and how you define *wall*), the Great Wall of China is somewhere between 5,500 to 14,000 miles long. A **mile** is 5,280 feet. That's 1.61 kilometers. A **kilometer** is simply 1,000 meters. In the metric system, base units, including meters, are given prefixes like *milli-*, *centi-*, and *kilo-*. Whatever unit you use, *milli-* means "thousandth," *centi-* means "hundredth," and *kilo-* means "thousand." So a kilometer is a thousand meters. Adding a prefix can take a metric unit all the way from a *yotta-*, or a septillion, to a *yocto-*, or a septillionth! (Still no word on how long the pandas think the wall is.)

ASTRONOMICAL UNIT

A unit of length used to measure distances in space, commonly abbreviated AU

The Sun doesn't revolve around the Earth, but we still see the universe from a very human perspective. When it comes to describing interstellar distances, we use a unit of measurement called an AU. An AU, or **astronomical unit**, is the distance from the Sun to the Earth, or 92,955,807 miles.

On average, we're about 1.0 AU away from the Sun. But since the Earth's orbit around the Sun isn't a perfect circle, sometimes we're a bit farther away. Mercury is .4 AU from the Sun. Neptune is 30.1 AU from the Sun. The farthest a spacecraft has traveled is just over 130 AU!

SATURN
URANUS
JUPITER
SUN
MERCURY
NEPTUNE
VENUS
1 AU
MARS
EARTH

LIGHT-YEAR & PARSEC

Units of length used to measure extremely long distances between planets, stars, and galaxies

Light-years are used to measure the mind-numbing distances between planets and stars. A light-year is equal to the distance light travels in a vacuum in one year. That's nearly 5.88 trillion miles!

A **parsec** is even bigger. Equal to 3.26 light-years, it's used to measure distances between stars and galaxies. Scientists think the universe is somewhere between 15 and 30 billion parsecs wide, which could make "Take me to your leader" a hard order to follow!

PROXIMA CENTAURI, THE CLOSEST STAR BEYOND OUR SUN, IS OVER 4.2 LIGHT-YEARS AWAY FROM EARTH.

VOLUME & MASS

How much stuff is there, and how much space does it take up? Everything from spoons to scales may be called on to answer this question. If you don't know your nonsense, it's easy to confuse volume, mass, and weight.

Most people talk about them as if they were the same thing. But **volume** measures the amount of space that is filled by a solid, liquid, or gas, and **mass** measures the amount of stuff an object contains. Weight measures the intensity of the force of gravity on an object. Confused? Don't worry. We'll explain shortly!

LIQUID MEASUREMENT

Units of volume used to measure the size of a container

A **gallon** isn't just the size of a milk container. A gallon can be used to measure how much space all kinds of solids, liquids, and gases take up. It's equal to four **quarts**. There are two **pints** in a quart. A **pint** is 16 **liquid ounces** or about the size of a tall glass of milk. In the metric system, a **liter** is the basic unit for measuring liquids, and it's about the same size as a quart. Got all that? Don't worry. When it comes to milk, any amooooount tastes good!

GALLON   QUART   PINT

IN THE KITCHEN

Units of volume used to measure small quantities in cooking

When you're in the kitchen, a little of this and a lot of that can lead to some delicious meals. But to avoid an inedible disaster, it helps to remember the difference between a **teaspoon** (tsp) and a **tablespoon** (tbsp). The abbreviations may look alike, but a teaspoon is about the size of the spoons you eat with, while a tablespoon is three times bigger. A **pinch** is just what it sounds like: the amount you can grab or break off with your finger and thumb.

3 TEASPOONS = 1 TABLESPOON

POUND

A unit of weight used to measure the pull of gravity on an object

Weight is easy to understand when you're using a scale. Heavy things weigh more than lighter things. But what's really being measured? **Pounds** measure the pull of gravity on an object. When you're weighing objects on Earth, you're measuring Earth's pull on the objects. Because the pull of gravity depends on the size of the planet you're measuring an object on, an object's weight varies depending where you measure it. That means if an elephant weighs 6,000 pounds on Earth, on a large planet like Jupiter, it would weigh even more. 15,162 pounds to be precise. Eek!

AN ENORMOUS ELEPHANT WEIGHS 6,000 POUNDS ON EARTH.

A MEEK MOUSE WEIGHS LESS THAN A POUND ON EARTH.

GRAM

A unit of mass used to measure the amount of matter in an object

Like weight, you measure mass on a scale, but what you're measuring is different. Mass isn't tied to a place or size. You can measure it on Jupiter, on the Moon, or back here on Earth, and the number never changes. A **gram** is the base metric unit of mass, or how much stuff is in an object.

Ready for more nonsense? You can't guess the mass of something based on its size. You can have two balls that are both the same size, but have different masses—like a bowling ball and a soccer ball. Can you guess which one has more mass? Typically, if it feels heavier, it has more mass.

MOLE

A number used to measure large quantities of atoms, molecules, and other particles, also spelled *mol*

In chemistry, a **mole** is a number, not an animal, and it's always the same number: 6.022×10^{23}. That's 602,000,000,000,000,000,000,000! Just like a dozen is 12 of whatever you're counting, a mole is 6.022×10^{23} of whatever you're measuring. It could be 6.022×10^{23} donuts, microbes, or anything else you can count, but when you're talking about moles, you're probably measuring atoms, molecules, or other small particles. Still not sure how much a mole is? There's a mole of water molecules in the amount you swallow when you take a drink of water. Gulp!

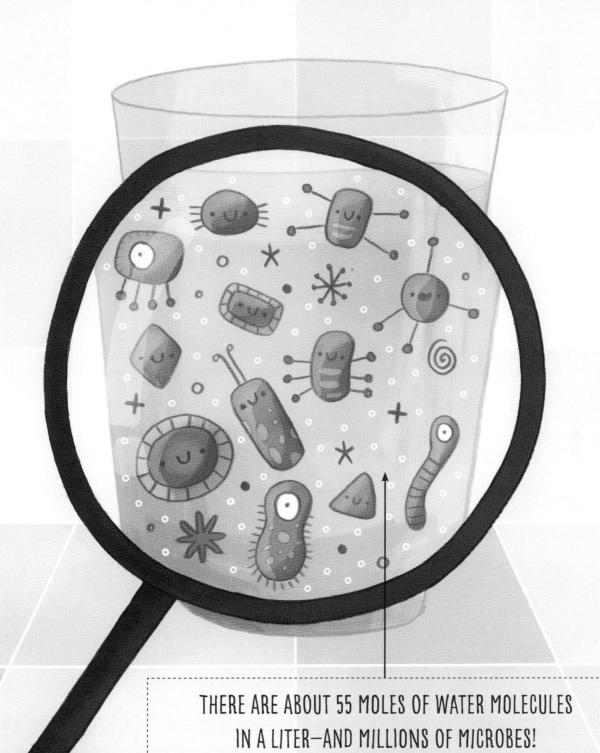

THERE ARE ABOUT 55 MOLES OF WATER MOLECULES
IN A LITER—AND MILLIONS OF MICROBES!

BITS & BYTES

Units used to measure amounts of information

Beep. Boop. Bop. We can't see it, but even information can be measured. A **bit** is the smallest unit of measurement for digital information. It can have a binary value of either 0 or 1, the digital equivalent of a yes or a no. It makes information as simple as possible and gives computers the choice between two possible outcomes. A **byte** is the amount of information that can be stored in a group of 8 bits. A byte is often used to stand for a letter or a number. For example, the lowercase letter "a" is 01100001. A 500-word essay is about 3,000 bytes of information. Just remember, these units don't measure the quality of the information. You could find yourself faced with gigabytes of total nonsense!

8 BITS = 1 BYTE
1,024 BYTES = 1 KILOBYTE (KB)
1,024 KB = 1 MEGABYTE (MB)
1,024 MB = 1 GIGABYTE (GB)
1,024 GB = 1 TERABYTE (TB)

TIME

How long does it take? Clocks, stopwatches, calendars, and even tree rings all measure how much time has passed. The unit you use depends on how much time you're measuring. Still have questions? Time to read on!

SECOND, MINUTE & HOUR

Units used to measure brief periods of time

There are 60 **seconds** in a minute, 60 **minutes** in an hour, and 24 **hours** in a day. Each is exactly as long as the last—although it doesn't always feel that way. Waiting for the clock to chime at midnight can feel like it takes forever, and a party with friends might make the hours fly by. If you're longing to show off your best moves under the disco ball, time just might feel like it's standing still. But rest assured! Tick, tock, tick, tock…keep your eye on the clock, and you'll see it never stops.

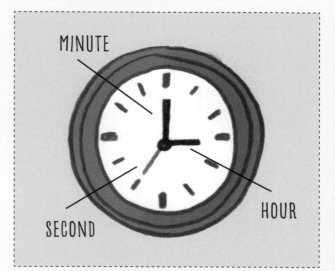

DAY, WEEK & MONTH

Units used to measure longer periods of time

Sunrise, sunset…every day, the Earth rotates all the way around the Sun once. The process takes 24 hours, or a **day**. There are 7 days in a **week** and roughly 4 weeks in a month. A **month** is the amount of time it takes the Moon to orbit the Earth, or about 30 days. But you don't have to visualize the solar system to count down to an exciting date. It can all be tracked on a calendar. Doing it in red pen is totally optional—but more dramatic!

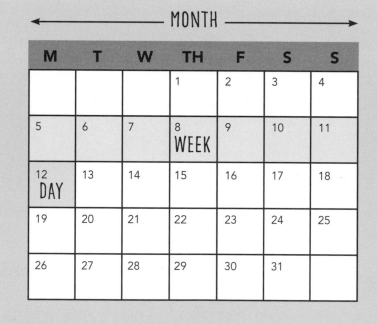

			MONTH			
M	**T**	**W**	**TH**	**F**	**S**	**S**
			1	2	3	4
5	6	7	8 WEEK	9	10	11
12 DAY	13	14	15	16	17	18
19	20	21	22	23	24	25
26	27	28	29	30	31	

FORTNIGHT

A unit of time that is 14 days long

Wimbledon, the grand tennis match, lasts a **fortnight**, or two weeks. The word comes from an old English word *fourtenight* or *fourtene night*, which means "fourteen nights." It's used more in Europe than in America, but even Yanks are beginning to use this uber specific unit when a **week** is too short and a **month** is too long. Game, set, match? The real winner in this tournament is precision!

M	T	W	TH	F	S	S
			1	2	3	4
5	6	7	8	9	10	11
12	13	14	15	16	17	18
19	20	21	22	23	24	25
26	27	28	29	30	31	

FORTNIGHT

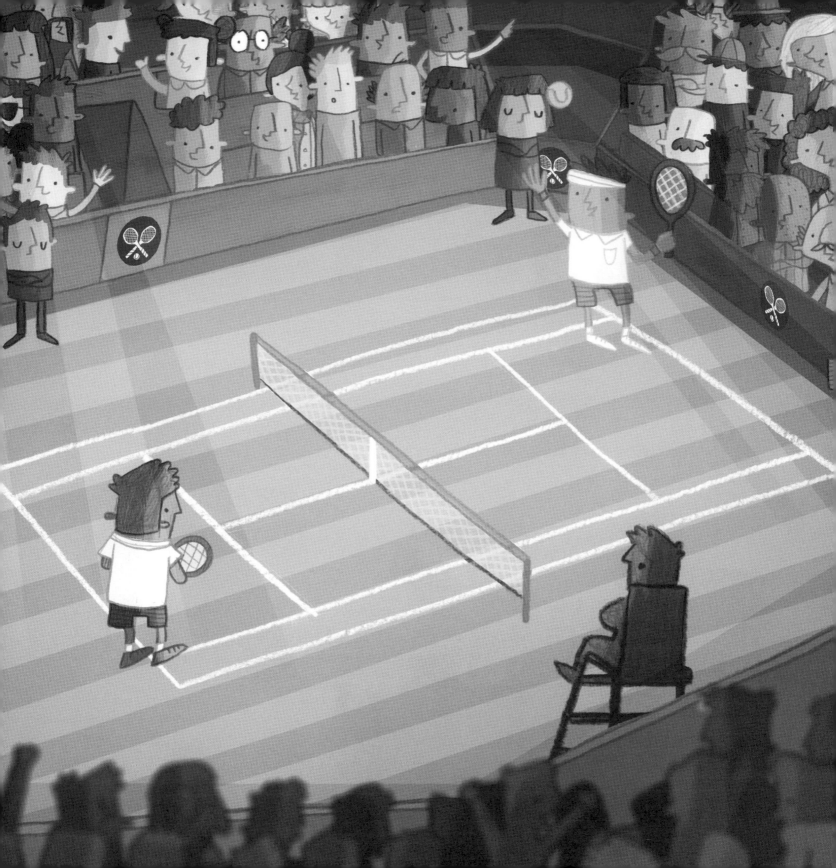

TREE RING

The amount a tree grows in one year

Whether they are wee saplings or grand old masters, as trees grow taller, each year they also grow a ring of cells inside. In spring, the trunk quickly grows a light layer of wood. In summer, a darker layer appears as a ring around the lighter wood. When a tree falls, scientists count the rings to learn how old the tree was. Each ring represents a year. **Tree rings** also reveal what the weather was like as the plant was growing. Drier seasons lead to narrower rings. When there's lots of rain and sunshine, rings are broad and even, a bit like the tree version of a leisurely sigh.

28 YEARS

7 YEARS

EPIC TIME SCALES

Units used to measure long periods of time

Humans have wandered the Earth for thousands of years. Ever since then, we've been tracking the passage of time, first with the Sun, then with calendars, atomic clocks, and even by stretching our imaginations far into the future.

There are 365 days in a **year**, 100 years in a **century**, and 1,000 years in a **millennium**. But when you start measuring time beyond human history, it makes sense to count in **eons**. This geological unit measures changes in the Earth, solar system, and beyond in billions of years. Pretty epic!

MILLIONS OF YEARS AGO

THOUSANDS OF YEARS AGO

HUNDREDS OF YEARS AGO

TODAY

INTENSITY

How strong is it? The tools and units you use to answer this question depend on the quality you're measuring.

The **force**, **energy**, **feeling**, or **strength** of an event or object can vary from so weak we barely notice it to hair-raisingly intense. Seismographs, thermometers, voltmeters, and even your tongue can tell you how powerful something is. And the results can be shocking!

RICHTER SCALE

A system used to measure the strength of an earthquake

The Earth may seem solid and steady, but sometimes it will shake, roll, and quake. When seismic waves of energy burst through the Earth's crust, it can cause the ground to shake and tsunamis to form in the ocean. The **Richter Scale** measures how much energy is released. Every day, thousands of earthquakes occur too low on the Richter scale to notice. The smallest earthquake that can be felt by people is a 1.5. Around a 4.0, an earthquake might cause slight damage, with pictures dropping off the walls and knickknacks breaking. And there's no way to miss an 8.0 on the Richter scale. An earthquake that size would do more than make a splash. It would be devastating. The good news is no earthquake above a 9.0 has been recorded. Cowabunga!

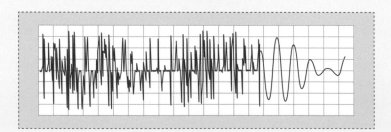

DECIBEL

A unit used to measure how loud a sound is

Psst! A **decibel** is a unit that measures how loud a sound is. Zero decibels is the threshold of human hearing. Anything softer is too quiet to be heard. A whisper is a mere 30 decibels. Most people talk around 60 decibels. An electric saw clocks in at 100 decibels. Crank it up and a rock concert might be 120 decibels. But not all sounds are created equal. Loud high-pitched sounds like a train screeching at 95 decibels makes us cover our ears, while lower pitches like a drummer at 95 decibels may inspire us to dance. Rock on!

NOISE LEVELS BY DECIBELS	
PNEUMATIC PRECISION DRILL	119
HAMMER DRILL	114
CHAIN SAW	110
SPRAY PAINTER	105
HAND DRILL	98
RECOMMENDED EXPOSURE LIMIT	85
NORMAL CONVERSATION	60
WHISPER	30

SCOVILLE SCALE

A system used to measure the spiciness of foods

If you're brave, the only tool you need to measure the Scoville rating of a jalapeño pepper is your tongue. The **Scoville Scale** rates the relative spiciness of foods. Everything from Tabasco sauce (2,500–5,000) to habanero peppers (100,000–350,000) is measured in SHU, or **Scoville heat units**. The measurement reflects how much water you need to drink to stop tasting how spicy something is. So if you drink a cup of hot sauce with a Scoville rating of 5,000, you'll need to drink 5,000 cups of water to no longer feel the heat. Ready to test your tongue? Better suit up. Anyone who dares to eat hot sauce with a 16-million rating on the Scoville Scale must wear gloves and goggles. *Yowza!*

SCOVILLE RATING CHART
BELL PEPPER: 0-100 SHU
SRIRACHA SAUCE: 2,200 SHU
TABASCO SAUCE: 2,500-5,000 SHU
JALAPEÑO PEPPER: 2,500-8,000 SHU
CHIPOTLE PEPPER: 5,000-10,000 SHU
HABANERO PEPPER: 100,000-350,000 SHU
GHOST PEPPER: 855,000-1,041,429 SHU

F-SCALE

A system used to measure the strength of a tornado

When a tornado hits, you don't want to be anywhere near it, so it can be tricky to measure how fast the wind is blowing. The **F-Scale** works backward and classifies how strong a tornado is by looking at how much damage it caused. It's only an estimate, but it's a good guess. F-0 tornadoes cause light damage. Winds are somewhere over 70 miles per hour and might knock some branches off trees. At the F-1 level, winds get closer to 100 miles per hour, and cars could be blown off the road. F-2 and F-3 tornadoes can lift cars and trains off the ground. Only 1 percent of tornadoes are an F-4 or higher. At over 260 miles per hour, F-5 tornadoes can send trucks and even houses flying up, up, and away over 100 meters!

SCALE	DAMAGE
F0	LIGHT
F1	MODERATE
F2	CONSIDERABLE
F3	SEVERE
F4	DEVASTATING
F5	INCREDIBLE

CELSIUS, FAHRENHEIT & KELVIN

Units used to measure temperature

No matter where you are, **Celsius** (°C), **Fahrenheit** (°F), and **Kelvin** (°K) are all different ways of measuring temperature, or how hot or cold something is. The units are named after the scientists who developed each method. The Kelvin scale starts at absolute zero, the point when atoms and molecules are almost completely still or frozen in place. As molecules begin to move more quickly, temperatures rise. Ice turns into water, and water turns into gas. Whatever you're measuring, you can find the temperature on all three scales. For example, water boils at 373K, 100°C, and 212°F. Most people use Celsius. Americans use Fahrenheit. Scientists use Kelvin. And birds? They fly south for the winter—it's warmer.

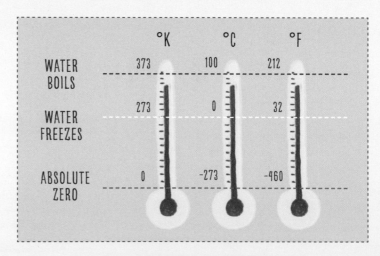

	°K	°C	°F
WATER BOILS	373	100	212
WATER FREEZES	273	0	32
ABSOLUTE ZERO	0	-273	-460

SOUTH POLE

-15 °F / -26 °C

100 °F / 38 °C

EQUATOR

TO CONVERT CELSIUS TO
FAHRENHEIT AND BACK AGAIN,
USE THIS FORMULA:
$$T(°F) = T(°C) \times \frac{9}{5} + 32$$

WINDCHILL

A unit used to measure how cold the air feels when it's windy

The air may be too warm for rain to freeze into snow, but the weather can still feel freezing. Wind draws heat from our skin, so the air feels colder. The stronger the wind, the faster it cools our skin—that's **windchill**. Scientists agree that when the windchill drops below -16°F, it's best to head indoors to avoid freezing skin. A weather station in Antarctica once recorded a windchill close to -150°F. No wonder the idea of the windchill factor was invented by Antarctic explorers!

WINDCHILL CHART

	OUTSIDE TEMPERATURE (°F)		
WIND SPEED (MPH)	40	0	-40
10	34	-16	-66
20	30	-22	-74
30	28	-26	-80
40	27	-29	-84
50	26	-31	-88
60	25	-33	-91

FROSTBITE TIMES

| 30 MINUTES | 10 MINUTES | 5 MINUTES |

CANDELA

A unit used to measure the intensity of light

If you manage to live to 100, you will be staring back at some serious candle power on your cake! A hundred candles produces 100 candelas of light. That's enough to light up your face (but not so bright that everyone will see all your wrinkles). A single candle produces about 1 **candela** of light. Why name a unit after a candle? Partly because candles have been around a lot longer than flashlights. And unlike a flashlight, which focuses the light, a candle shines in all directions. The formula used to calculate the exact amount of light gets pretty intense—green wavelengths, molten platinum, and some serious math are all involved. The important thing to know is a candela measures how strong a light is at its source. Now make a wish!

100 CANDELAS

1 CANDELA

VOLT

A unit used to measure the force that moves an electric current

Zzzap! Electricity is a type of energy that can build up and move from place to place—even the human body. It flows like water. The force behind the current is measured in **volts**. The more you increase the voltage, the more current will flow—and the more power you'll get. Wall sockets in the United States release 120 volts. But nature can be even more shocking. Electric eels use 600 volts to paralyze their prey. And a lightning bolt can shoot a billion volts to the ground!

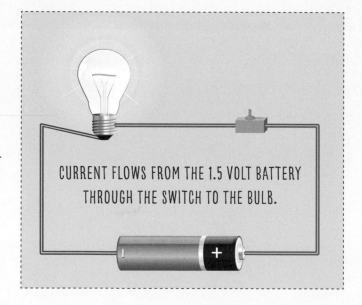

CURRENT FLOWS FROM THE 1.5 VOLT BATTERY THROUGH THE SWITCH TO THE BULB.

A NOTE TO KNOW-IT-ALLS

Now that you've measured everything from parsecs to pints, use these know-nonsense guides to master the finer points of measurement and show off what a know-it-all you are now.

CONVERSIONS

Use this chart to find equivalencies in the US and metric systems.

	Unit	American	SI
Length	Inch (in)	12 inches = 1 foot	1 inch = 2.54 centimeters or .0254 meter
	Foot (ft)	3 feet = 1 yard	1 foot = .3048 meter
	Meter (m)	1 meter = 3.28084 feet	1 meter = 100 centimeters
	Yard (yd)	1,760 yards = 1 mile	1 yard = .9144 meter
	Mile (mi)	1 mile = 5,280 feet	1 mile = 1.60934 kilometers
Volume	Fluid ounce (fl oz)	8 fluid ounces = 1 cup	1.5 fluid ounces = 45 milliliters
	Cup (c)	2 cups = 1 pint	1 cup = 237 milliliters
	Pint (pt)	2 pints = 1 quart	1 pint = 473 milliliters
	Liter (L)	1 liter = 1.05669 quarts	1 liter = 1,000 milliliters
	Quart (qt)	4 quarts = 1 gallon	1 quart = 946 milliliters
	Gallon (gal)	1 gallon = 16 cups	1 gallon = 3.78541 liters
	Teaspoon (tsp)	3 teaspoons = 1 tablespoon	1 teaspoon = 4.92892 milliliters
	Tablespoon (tbsp)	16 tablespoons = 1 cup	2 tablespoons = 1 ounce
Weight & Mass	Pound (lb)	1 pound = 16 ounces	1 pound = 453.592 grams (on Earth)
	Gram (g)	1 gram = .03527 ounces	1 gram = 1,000 milligrams

TIME

Use this chart to convert between units of time.

60 seconds	= 1 minute
60 minutes	= 1 hour
24 hours	= 1 day
7 days	= 1 week
4 weeks	= 1 month
12 months	= 1 year
10 years	= 1 decade
100 years	= 1 century
10 centuries	= 1 millennium

PREFIXES

Use these prefixes with base units to make very small and very large numbers easier to work with.

Multiply By	SI Prefix	Scientific Notation
1 000 000 000 000	tera (T)	10^{12}
1 000 000 000	giga (G)	10^{9}
1 000 000	mega (M)	10^{6}
1 000	kilo (k)	10^{3}
0.001	milli (m)	10^{-3}
0.000 001	micro (μ)	10^{-6}
0.000 000 001	nano (n)	10^{-9}
0.000 000 000 001	pico (p)	10^{-12}

ALSO IN THIS SERIES

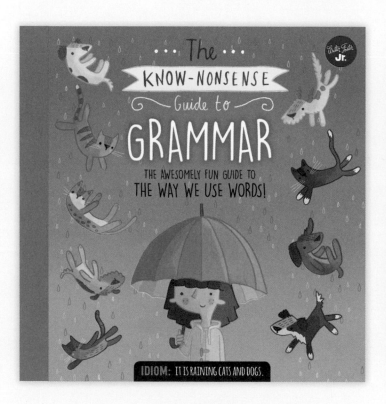

COMING NOVEMBER 2017

Full of quirky and hilarious illustrations, *The Know-Nonsense Guide to Grammar* teaches basic concepts about grammar, including alliteration, similes, hyperbole, and more.

Full of quirky and hilarious illustrations, *The Know-Nonsense Guide to Money* teaches basic concepts about money, including smart saving, counting, different currencies, and more.